CW00918531

Ned Ludd & Queen Mab

Machine-Breaking, Romanticism, and the Several Commons of 1811–12

For David F. Noble
1945–2010

RETORT Pamphlet Series

Titles in the Retort Pamphlet Series

Note from the Author

This pamphlet began as a lecture at a bicentennial conference called "The Luddites, without Condescension" held at Birkbeck College, University of London, May 6, 2011, and a précis was subsequently offered at a conference held in Amsterdam, June 16–18, 2011, called "Mutiny and Maritime Radicalism during the Age of Revolution: A Global Survey." I thank Iain Boal and Marcus Rediker for inviting me to these two occasions. Niklas Frykman, Forrest Hylton, David Lloyd, Charles Beattie-Medina, Gordon Bigelow, Manuel Yang, and Colin Thomas provided helpful suggestions.

Cover and book design
Lisa Thompson, duckdogdesign.com

Cover Illustration
Inés Chapela

Retort Logo Design
Lori Fagerholm, lorifagerholm.blogspot.com

Retort Pamphlet Series No. 001
Ned Ludd & Queen Mab
Peter Linebaugh
ISBN: 978-1-60486-704-6

Peter Linebaugh © 2012
All photographs and images have their source in the public domain.

This edition copyright 2012 PM Press
All Rights Reserved

PM Press
PO Box 23912
Oakland, CA 94623
www.pmpress.org

Printed in Oakland, CA, on recycled paper with soy ink.

THE RETORT PAMPHLET SERIES

The Retort Pamphlet series marks a collaboration between Retort and PM Press.

Retort is a gathering of writers, artists, artisans, teachers, filmmakers, scientists, and motley antinomians, drawn together in a sustaining web of friendship now crossing generations and all sharing an antagonism to capital and empire. The group—it is not a collective, there are no members—has its origins and heart in the San Francisco Bay Area, but after two and a half decades, being no respecters of borders, the range of our collaborations is far-reaching.

In a world of the witless txt and abbreviated attention, we nevertheless remain partisans of the short form. One major collaboration, *Afflicted Powers: Capital and Spectacle in a New Age of War*, which emerged from the 2003 broadside *Neither Their War Nor Their Peace*, was conceived as a pamphlet, and was referred to as such long after it grew too bulky to be stapled into one signature. "The book's stance," we said, "is deliberately polemical, in the tradition (we hope) of the pamphleteering characteristic of the Left in its heyday. On occasion we turned aside in the course of our writing—for encouragement, but also to remind ourselves sadly of what once was possible—to read a few pages from Rosa Luxemburg's great *Junius Brochure* or Randolph Bourne's *The State*." We found inspiration, too, in the poetry and pamphlets of Milton, and in the ferocity of the leveling antinomians freed to write following the breakdown of censorship in the revolutionary decades of the seventeenth century. Retort's style, wrote one critic, is "venomous and poetic." No higher praise.

In taking the name Retort we were gesturing in part to an earlier publishing venture, the nonsectarian 1940s journal of that title printed in a cabin in Bearsville, New York, on a press that had belonged to the eloquent Wobbly agitator Carlo Tresca before he was assassinated on the streets of Manhattan. The journal was antistatist, antimilitarist and published essays on art, politics, and culture. Poetry too—the first issue included the Kenneth Rexroth poem that begins, "Now in Waldheim where the rain/ Has fallen careless and unthinking/ For all an evil century's youth, / Where now the banks of dark roses lie…" From Holly Cantine's press also came *Prison Etiquette: The Convict's Compendium of Useful Information*, compiled by war resisters, specifically those imprisoned for refusing to collaborate either with the state or with the Anabaptist "peace churches" who had agreed with the U.S. government to self-manage the rural work camps for conscientious objectors.

The name also acknowledges that we are engaged in a wider conversation whose terms and assumptions we reject, and that we stand on ground, rhetorical and otherwise, not of our own choosing. We are forced to spend far too much time…retorting. Some of the pamphlets in the series will—who doubts it?—have to be composed in this mode, hastily, to the occasion, and as an immediate practical response to some new tragi-comic episode in the barbarisms currently on offer. Others will aim to clear ground, to open up views, to push on with the hard work of root-and-branch rethinking of the terms and tactics necessary under the new conditions of life in the rubble of the twentieth century. The themes of the pamphlets will no doubt range as widely as the interests of Retort's motley crew—history, science, art, politics, the image world, technics, and more. We realize that sometimes their instrumentality, their time as a weapon, may lie a little in the future. However, as reading matter all will be equally handy and at home in old cafes and city taverns, on beaches and river banks, in the bleachers or the back country. No batteries needed.

Finally, the logo of PM's new imprint sets resonating that older sense of retort, the alchemist's lovely, fragile vessel that—with enough heat applied from below—ferments, distills, and transforms.

Ned Ludd & Queen Mab has its origins in an address by Peter Linebaugh at a conference entitled "The Luddites, without Condescension" and convened at Birkbeck, "home of lost causes," to mark the two-hundredth anniversary of the uprising of the handloom weavers in 1811. Historians, veteran campaigners, and some young antagonists of the present gathered to reflect on E.P. Thompson's declared ambition, in the famous preface to *The Making of the English Working Class*, to rescue the Luddites from "the enormous condescension of posterity," and in the course of the day to debate contemporary exponents of the tactics of direct action—antinuclear warriors, environmental monkey-wrenchers, road resisters, GM crop saboteurs. In the closing session T.J. Clark addressed the issue of modernity itself, its future-orientation, and modes of resistance to it.

At a moment of disillusionment Edward Thompson, looking back over the years spent in the archives, felt his work in English social history parochial and trivial; "as the last imperial illusions of the twentieth century fade, so preoccupation with the history and culture of a small island off the coast of Europe becomes open to the charge of narcissism." No longer. *Ned Ludd & Queen Mab* with one stroke rescues E.P. Thompson from the charge of insular narcissism and rescues the Luddites from the charge of backward-facing irrelevance. The myth of Ludd and the spirit of Mab, as Linebaugh tells it, are imaginative local defenses in a world of artisans and commoners mobilizing against mechanization for profit and planetary enclosures.

Sadly, David Noble, historian of the "machinery question" (or as we would now say, "technology") and author of *Progress without People: In Defense of Luddism*, died very soon after accepting the invitation to launch the proceedings in Bloomsbury that he would have graced with his fearless, critical spirit and a deep knowledge of the forces of production and their role in human history. *Ned Ludd & Queen Mab* is dedicated to David's memory.

ACKNOWLEDGEMENTS

Thanks are due to Julie Eisner, Esther Leslie, Anna Davin, and Tom 'Dangerous to Know' Smith for his performance of Byron's maiden speech in defense of the Luddites against the bill that made the breaking of frames a hanging offense. IB

ABOUT THE AUTHOR

Peter Linebaugh is a child of empire, schooled in London, Cattaraugus, N.Y., Washington D.C., Bonn, and Karachi. He went to Swarthmore College during the civil rights days. He has taught at Harvard University and Attica Penitentiary, at New York University and the Federal Penitentiary in Marion, Illinois. He used to edit *Zerowork* and was a member of the Midnight Notes Collective. He coauthored *Albion's Fatal Tree*, and is the author of *The London Hanged*, *The Many-Headed Hydra* (with Marcus Rediker), *The Magna Carta Manifesto*, and introductions to a Verso book of Thomas Paine's writing and PM's new edition of E.P. Thompson's *William Morris: Romantic to Revolutionary*. He works at the University of Toledo, Ohio. He lives in the Great Lakes region with a great crew, Michaela Brennan, his beautiful partner, and Riley, Kate, Alex, and Enzo.

PETER LINEBAUGH

No General but Ludd
Means the Poor Any Good
—ANONYMOUS, *1811–12*

I.

The economic term *constant capital* denotes both natural resources and machines, or Nature and Technology, as means for the exploitation of *variable capital*, the term for the working class when it is waged or unwaged, or labor-power either employed or unemployed.

The *system* of capitalism begins to collapse when labor power expresses itself as the power of the people and attacks the machines of its degradation and resumes responsibility for the earth. We may do this in the name of democracy or popular sovereignty, or we may do this in the name of human dignity and survival. Both are now required. The 2011 natural disasters of earthquake, tsunami, tornado, and fire are inseparable from the artificial catastrophes of global warming and the nuclear meltdown.

The popular mobilization in Cairo, the Tahrir Square commons, raised hopes of the oppressed struggling for rights they never had. In Madison, Wisconsin, the workers took over the state capitol struggling for rights they were about to lose. The Fukushima disaster gave the whole world a jolt. The Occupation of Wall Street takes the system at its most abstract (banks) and exclusive (private property) and grounds it concretely and in common thus prefiguring the future in the present.

Everyone knows now that technology has brought us to an impasse, and everyone knows now that everything has to be looked at globally, though these commonplaces were not so generally known two hundred years ago when the world and the heavens were in uproar and the people in the name of "Ned Ludd" took up the hammer of redress to smash machines. The origin of the industrial *system* contains the seed of its demise, once we apply to it our hammers and our imagination which also appeared, fairy-like, two hundred years ago.

In 1811 it appeared to many that cosmic forces were at play. A great comet was visible for most of the year, 260 days, seen first in March, most visible in October, and faded by January 1812. Its tail was 25 degrees long. It was interpreted as an omen all over the world.

July 5, 1811, is Independence Day in Venezuela. Independence was led by Francisco de Miranda and Simón Bolívar. An earthquake shattered much in March 1812. Bolívar said, "If nature opposes us, we shall fight against her and force her to obey." The leaders of the bourgeois revolution were prepared to conquer nature.

December 16, 1811, a terrific earthquake shook the grounds of the central Mississippi River valley, and there were others in January and February. The earthquake brought justice to a murder committed by Thomas Jefferson's nephews who in Kentucky axed a slave, chopped up his body, and sought to burn the parts, until the earthquake caused the chimney to collapse smothering the fire leaving the body parts visible to others.[1] Among the Creek, indigenous people of the American south, the Red Stick prophets had begun to urge young braves to follow Tecumseh and prepare themselves for the war path. Tecumseh and his brother Tenskatawa welcomed the association with the earthquake.

Meanwhile in England Anna Laetitia Barbauld published a volume, a poem, called *Eighteen Hundred and Eleven*. Generally known for introducing big letters and wide margins to help children read, she saw history with two eyes, chronology and geography, which provided her with prophetic power. The war, famine, rapine, disease of the year brought catastrophe and the eruption of subterranean forces. "Ruin, as with an earthquake shock, is here," she warned.

Frank Peel in 1878 provided the first primary, printed source of authentic memories of the Luddites. On the first page he compared the comet to "a flaming sword."[2] Only a few years before the Luddites William Blake wrote a hymn against the mechanized factory, "these dark Satanic Mills," in which he vowed,

> *I will not Cease from mental Fight*
> *Nor shall my Sword sleep in my hand*
> *Till we have built Jerusalem*
> *In England's green and pleasant Land.*

1. I am grateful to Jesse Olavasky for bringing this crime to my attention. See Marion B. Lucas, *A History of Blacks in Kentucky: From Slavery to Segregation, 1760–1891*, (Lexington, KY: The Kentucky Historical Society, 1992), 47–48.
2. Frank Peel, *The Risings of the Luddites*, 4th ed. with an introduction by E.P. Thompson (London: Cass, 1968), 1.

Had the sleeping sword awakened? Were the followers of Ned Ludd, like the comet in the sky, wielding cosmic justice and do they still? If so, it was not as Blake imagined because Jerusalem, a city of strife and division, is no longer the egalitarian utopia of the Protestant millennium. An ecological rather than the protestant nationalist note must now conclude this stirring and beautiful hymn.

> *I will not Cease from mental Fight*
> *Nor shall my Sword sleep in my hand*
> *Till we occupy the Commons*
> *To green and chill our baked Lands.*

On the bicentennial of the Luddite direct actions on behalf of commonality, the chthonic powers beneath the earth and the cosmic spectacle above it accompanied the revolt against the machine. The Romantic poets responded to this relationship in two ways. First, they broadened our view from the local to the revolutionary macrocosm. Second, they helped make it possible to see machine-breaking as a means of defending the commons.

II.

The Luddites were machine-breakers of the north of England who differed from tool-breakers of the past or of other countries by giving themselves a mythological name, Ned Ludd, or Captain Ludd. The Luddites were active in three areas of the English textile industry: i) the West Riding of Yorkshire where the croppers (those who shear, or crop, the nap of the cloth) were threatened by the gig-mill or shearing machine, ii) Nottinghamshire and adjacent parts of the midlands where the stockingers (those who weave stockings) were being made redundant by the framework-knitting machine, and iii) Lancashire where the cotton weavers were losing employment because of the application of the steam-engine to the hand-loom. This area has been called "the Luddite triangle." The main Luddite resistance took place in 1811 and 1812.

Both the general tactic of machine-breaking and its specific most famous case of Luddism, may indeed be "collective bargaining by riot," to

George Walker's Costume of Yorkshire (1814) illustrates the hidden transcript of Ludism. Step one: a community of women and children collect teasels in the commons,

Step two: while men raise the nap ("rooing") a boy detaches flocks from used teasels, showing that artisans controlled apprenticeship,

Step three: four darkly handsome croppers take their time as the boss tentatively surveils the cut, his stick in hand.

use the phrase of E.J. Hobsbawm, but there was more to them than that.[3] "I am seeking rescue the poor stockinger, the Luddite cropper, the 'obsolete' hand-loom weaver, the 'utopian' artisan, and even the deluded follower of Joanna Southcott from the enormous condescension of posterity," wrote E.P. Thompson in *The Making of the English Working Class* (1963). The first three figures (stockinger, cropper, weaver) are the three crafts corresponding to the three regions of Luddism and to three machines that were undermining them. To Thompson three of these five examples were machine-breakers, suggesting an identification between them and the class of all working people. The prefigurative power of a chronologically specific tactic found expression as myth, and since myth may transcend the time and place of its birth, Ned Ludd continues to wield his hammer centuries later.

Such mythological figures, like the porter in *Macbeth*, open the gates to history from below. English history is replete with them—Robin Hood, Piers Ploughman, Lady Skimmington, Captain Swing for example—and so is Irish history especially in this period (1811–12) when Captain Knockabout or Captain Rock joined Ned Ludd as anonymous, avenging avatars who meted out justice that was otherwise denied.

The world was being enclosed, life was being closed off, people shut in. In 1795 before he was silenced by government the English Jacobin, John Thelwall, referred to "the inclosing system" which he defined as "that system of enclosure by which the rich monopolize to themselves the estates, rights, and possessions of the poor."[4]

Certainly the system of enclosure applied to land where enclosure became commodification. In 1790 there were 25 Parliamentary Enclosure Acts, and in 1811 there were 133. England began to become a country of fences, stone walls, ditches, and hedges. To Barbauld, writing in *Eighteen Hundred and Eleven*, "stricter bounds the cultured fields divide." The result on one side was high rents and Jane Austen and on the other dispossession, hunger, and John Clare, the Northamptonshire agricultural laborer and poet of the commons, who wrote, "vile enclosure came and made / A parish slave of me."

The household became part of the system of enclosure. The genders were separated by the doctrine of the two spheres, the private sphere for women

3. E.J. Hobsbawm, *Labouring Men: Studies in the History of Labour* (New York: Basic Books, 1964).
4. Report on the State of Popular Opinion and Causes of the Increase of Democratic Principles, *The Tribune* 28 (September 1795).

and the public sphere for men. "The confines of the home were the boundaries of her kingdom," writes Linda Colley. The wife ceased to have a legal *persona* or existence.[5] The cult of prolific maternity was to supply cannon-fodder for empire. The "population explosion" was partly an achievement of this confinement or lying-in.

The division of labor in the arts and crafts enabled them to become part of the system of enclosure as the factory replaced the workshop. The resulting dehumanization was anticipated in Adam Smith's *Wealth of Nations*: "In the progress of the division of labor, the employment . . . of the great body of the people, comes to be confined to a few very simple operations, frequently to one or two. The man whose whole life is spent in performing a few simple operations . . . generally becomes as stupid and ignorant as it is possible for a human creature to become."[6]

The infrastructures of transportation belong to the enclosing system. Rivers were canalized and high dock walls enclosed the traffic of ports from Liverpool to London. The result was criminalization. In punishment it was an age of vast prison construction behind immense walls of granite. Lord Byron in defending the Luddites asked the legislators, "Can you commit a whole country to their own prisons?"

War itself assisted the system of enclosure. The soldiers were separated from the civilian population by the replacement of billeting by barracks. More than two hundred barracks were constructed between 1799 and the end of the war in 1815. It was said in India that if the Moghuls built mosques and tombs the British built jails and barracks.[7] Even "Albion's fatal tree" or the three-mile procession of the condemned from the city of London to the Tyburn gallows was subject to enclosure at Newgate prison.

In cultural expressions, too, we find several forms of closure, such as the dictionaries and grammars of language, the censorship of press and speech, and the silencing of Thelwall, who spent the rest of his life relieving stammerers by teaching "elocution." Thomas Spence attempted to combat it by spelling reform but to no avail. The result contributed to that social and cul-

5. Linda Colley, *Britons*, 239, 256 ("In Great Britain, woman was subordinate and confined. But at least she was safe.").
6. Book V, chapter 1 in Adam Smith, *The Wealth of Nations* (1776), ed. Edwin Seligman, two vols. (London: Dent, 1958), ii, 264.
7. C.A. Bayly, *Imperial Meridian: The British Empire and the World, 1780–1830* (London: Longman, 1989), 129.

tural apartheid between the upper class and the common people. Indeed the word *common* became a slur.

The enclosure of handicraft started with the domestic system of the merchants putting out raw materials to the craftsman and the craftswoman working at home where the round of tasks in garden, field, and loom were industriously mixed. Then, manufactures or the separate workshop, brought all the workers together. The factory added machines and power. Enclosure depends on the separation of industry from agriculture, the factory from the land. The two processes were carried forward together. Enclosure destroyed both.

These enclosures took place in an era of world war and total war. In 1811–12, "an event took place," Tolstoy will say in *War and Peace*, "opposed to human reason and to human nature. Millions of men perpetrated against one another such innumerable crimes, frauds, treacheries, thefts, forgeries, issues of false money, burglaries, incendiarisms, and murders as in whole centuries are not recorded in the annals of all the law courts of the world, but which those who committed them did not at the time regard as being crimes."[8] As far as Britain was concerned this was a new phase in the long counterrevolution against liberty, equality, and fraternity and an opportunity to control the commerce of the Atlantic, Indian, and Pacific oceans. Its war economy and its industrialization went hand in hand: the smoke of the factory and the smoke of cannon, the hapless soldier's cry and the orphan's cry, vast fortunes and the fortunes of war, war and the machine morphed politically into the military-industrial complex.

The Americans still sing before sporting events a national anthem referring to the "rockets' red glare." Rockets were fired at Fort McHenry in Baltimore during the war of 1812. Rocketry was the advanced military technology of the day, originating in India at the battle of Seringapatam in 1799 and carefully studied by Robert Emmet in the insurrection of 1802. During this total war hundreds of thousands of soldiers put boots on the ground, boots made of hides from cattle fed in the pastures of Ireland or the pampas of Argentina. Pick any thread of this tapestry, pull it, and, yes, the historian unravels the cruelties and crimes of the era, but look more carefully and there is another story which sticks to the hand. It is the story of preservation, resistance, kind-

---

8. At the beginning of book nine.

ness to strangers, a seat at the table. This was the commons, and so it was with the Luddites.

David Noble's "In Defense of Luddism" (1993) like E.J. Hobsbawm's essay four decades earlier stressed the solidarity resulting from exercising power "at the point of production."[9] "The habit of solidarity, which is the foundation of effective trade unionism, takes time to learn," wrote Hobsbawm, and nothing does it better, than bringing production to a halt by machine-breaking or "to go out Ludding." By Noble's time in the late twentieth century the trade unions were cooperating in the introduction of automation. Since the permanence of capitalism can seem to rest on the inevitability of technological change, Noble called us to regain our inherently insurrectionary power with the reprise of Ned Ludd. More is at stake, however, than the "point of production." That point depends on reproduction, or the community of the producers.

When we speak of the destruction of "community" we must remember that this entailed complex kin patterns, forms of mutuality, and customs held in common. There is a material basis to community; together they constitute a commons. In both cases land and tools became commodities (they could be bought and sold) and the commodities became constant capital (a tangible means to increase of labor exploitation). In this way expropriation (X) and exploitation (X^1) became not separate stages of capitalism, as $X + X^1$, but an intensifying dynamic operating on one another simultaneously, as X^2. The expropriation from the commons and the mechanization of labor worked upon each other as in a feedback loop.

III.

We can introduce "the commons" by pulling an Irish thread—Ireland so close to England geographically, so distant otherwise. In 1811 from Ulster William Carleton set out for Munster in search of a teacher to teach him the classics of Greece and Rome. Irish people, poor or not, venerated classical learning. "Such was the respect held for those who appeared to be anxious to acquire education, that . . . I was not permitted to pay a farthing for either bed or board in the roadside houses of entertainment where

9. David Noble, *Progress without People: In Defense of Luddism* (Chicago: Charles H. Kerr Publishing Co., 1993).

I stopped." Eventually he found a teacher whose brother had just returned from the Iberian Peninsula with a Portuguese wife. They will eat potatoes.

In the Peninsula, however, the British Army ate bread. The Army bought grain from Malta where Egyptian wheat was unloaded. This was a major change in the international grain trade. Muhammad Ali routed the mameluk leadership at a feast in Cairo in March 1811, the first step in centralizing power in Egypt. The second step was the reorientation of the grain exports away from Ottoman markets via sea trade protected by the British Navy to meet needs of the British Army.[10] However other characteristics of "primitive accumulation" had commenced, the expropriation of charity and religiously endowed lands, centralization of taxes and tributes, and the privatization of lands, intensification of irrigation corvées, or forced labor on canals. In Upper Egypt lands were "held communally and assigned to individual cultivators annually" but in the fertile delta of lower Egypt boundaries were easily established.[11]

So, here's a change in Egypt: grain for a new, large market, which causes reduction in subsistence farming and removal of several forms of commoning. While these changes might help feed armies in the Iberian Peninsula, they could not feed the hungry bellies of England during this winter of shortages. George Mellor, the Yorkshire Luddite who was to hang in 1813, was a veteran of the British campaign in Egypt.

Scarcity was answered by the renewal of the moral economy in England and the persistence of "agrarian outrages" in Ireland against tithes, taxes, cesses, and high prices of land. Land for cattle grazing left the people hungry for land for food, which was available only by the system of conacre—a half acre, or potato patch, leased from sowing to harvest, rent paid by labor. These were the conditions for a flourishing legal subculture, or "the clear notion of a code of laws quite separate from that represented by government." The Rockites defended this legal subculture against law administered by Castle and court.

---

10. Muhammad Ali's state-sponsored long staple cotton industry did not begin until 1821. Afaf Lutfi Al-Sayyid Marsot, *Egypt in the Reign of Muhammad Ali* (Cambridge: Cambridge University Press, 1984), 145, and Henry Dodwell, *The Founder of Modern Egypt: A Study of Muhammad 'Ali* (Cambridge: Cambridge University Press, 1931), 32.
11. Alan Richards, *Egypt's Agricultural Development, 1800–1980: Technical and Social Change* (Boulder, CO: Westview Press, 1982), 12.

Here are a few examples of Irish anonymous letters from the Luddite years of 1811 and 1812. To a curate of Ardcolm, near Wexford, a letter writer advised him "to study Divinity and not oppression especially as you being well paid for it." A second warned, "Any person who will persevere in oppression let them expect nothing but emediate [sic] execution." A third warned against a ship owner from sailing away from co. Down with a load of potatoes who might receive a visit from Captain Slasher or Captain Firebrand, on behalf of "poor indigint peasants who lies fettered under the yoke of tyranny." Captain Knockabout might visit to cause the rents to fall.[12]

While studying the fourth book of Virgil's *Aeneid* and admiring Defoe's *History of the Devil*, William Carleton came upon a wedding dance upon the greensward and under the influence of poteen and a red-haired fellow who was "seldom absent in fair or market from a fight," a Catholic prayer-book was pressed into his hand, and he was given the words and signs of a Ribbonman swearing allegiance to an independent Ireland, to mutuality in defense against Orangemen, and to noncooperation with the courts.[13] This was part of the Irish Catholic "underground" with links to an older, commoning economy of land and labor.

IV.

In pulling an Irish thread, we incidentally came across several types of commons, including the knowledge commons supported by Irish hospitality and the very old agrarian commons of the Upper Nile as well as the Nile delta. Notions of community and of commons were central to the Luddites.

> We will never lay down Arms [till] The House of Commons passes
> an Act to put down all Machinery hurtful to Commonality, and repeal
> that to hang Frame Breakers. But We. We petition no more—that
> won't do—fighting must.
>> Signed by the General of the Army of Redressers
>> Ned Ludd Clerk
>> Redressers for ever. Amen

12. Stephen Randolph Gibbons, *Captain Rock, Night Errant: The Threatening Letters of Pre-Famine Ireland, 1801–1845* (Dublin: Four Courts Press, 2004), 59, 60.
13. *The Autobiography of William Carleton* (London: Macgibbon & Kee, 1968).

This was the conclusion to a long letter sent to Mr. Smith, a shearing-frame holder, in Hill End, Yorkshire, and made public on March 9, 1812. The letter warned that 2,782 people in Huddersfield alone were ready to destroy machines and burn the buildings of the frame holders. Furthermore the army of redressers came not only from Manchester, Halifax, Sheffield, Bradford, and Oldham, but the weavers of Glasgow were ready to join, and "the Papists in Ireland are rising to a Man." In addition "we hope for the assistance of the French Emperor in shaking off the Yoke of the Rottenest, Wickedest, and most Tyrannous Government that ever existed."[14]

Following the defeat of the Irish rebellion of '98 and its aftershocks including the Act of Union (1801), the Despard conspiracy (1802), and Emmet's revolt (1803) thousands of Irish immigrants fled for meager employment opportunities in Lancashire and the West Riding of Yorkshire. It was a crucial migratory movement to the textile factories whose spinners in 1811 struck demanding equal pay between the country and the city. Thirty thousand were thrown out of work; the factories were attacked. Despite their defeat in two or three years John Doherty of co. Donegal who himself had begun work as a child in a Belfast spinning mill would become one of the most successful trade union leaders of the era.[15]

The atmosphere of the time as felt by the gentry is described by Charlotte Brontë in her novel *Shirley* (1849) and by Emily Brontë in her novel *Wuthering Heights* (1847). The empty landscape and ominous turbulent weather which open *Wuthering Heights* indicate the terror and fear of the Other (Irish, Gypsy, proletarian). It is a shadowy representation of the actuality when the people of the north prepared for civil war by practicing military evolutions upon the moors by the light of the moon.

"Machinery hurtful to Commonality." This is the phrase that introduces our theme, the mixture of communism and commons against which the ma-

14. Kevin Binfield (ed.), *Writings of the Luddites* (Baltimore: Johns Hopkins University Press, 2004), 209–11. While my own knowledge of the Luddites begins with Thompson's *Making of the English Working Class* (1963) and Kirkpatrick Sale, *Rebels Against the Future: The Luddites and Their War on the Industrial Revolution: Lessons for the Computer Age* (New York: Addison-Wesley, 1995), recent local history enlarges our knowledge. Kartrina Navickas, "Luddism, Incendiarism and the Defence of Rural 'Task-Scapes' in 1812," *Northern History* 48, no. 1 (March 2011), deepens knowledge of the dual economy, farming, and textiles.
15. R.G. Kirby and A.E. Musson, *The Voice of the People: John Doherty, 1798–1854, Trade Unionist, Radical and Factory Reformer* (Manchester: Manchester University Press, 1975), 2, 14.

chine and enclosure were launched in all its dehumanizing consequences.[16] For those triplets of evil which Martin Luther King called militarism, racism, and materialism and which Milton personified as demons, Moloch, Belial, and Mammon were let loose upon the world's common, "hurtful to the commonality." Veritably, this was hell on earth.

Percy Bysshe Shelley was thrown out of Oxford for atheism in March 1811 and searching for a commune of equality he began a life-long quest, at first in the north of England, witnessing the extreme economic conditions of Lancashire and Yorkshire and tramping the commons, "over the cold and beautiful upland pastures" of the Lake District, and then, second, by a political intervention in Ireland where he went on February 12, 1812, staying until April 4. Shelley's poetic, political, and philosophical changes occurred at the peak of the Luddite disturbances.

At the same time as Ned Ludd sent his letter on behalf of the commonality Shelley, returning from political agitation in Ireland, composed a broadside

Percy Shelley, by Alfred Clint, 1819

to post on the walls of public buildings, *A Declaration of Rights* of thirty-one articles. Shelley sealed a copy in a bottle and lobbed it into the Bristol Channel, and launched another copy as "heavenly medicine" in a hot air balloon. The aristocratic whimsy of a blithe spirit? Yes, and something in addition, namely, wave and wind as media of communication. At Oxford in the spring of 1811 Shelley witnessed James Sadler, the aeronaut, ascend in a hot air balloon. Man could fly over Africa and "virtually emancipate every

16. W.B. Crump (ed.), *The Leeds Woollen Industry, 1780–1820* (Leeds: Thoresby Society, 1931), 229–30.

slave," thought Shelley. The thought was not as far-fetched as it might seem.
In 1812 Sadler attempted to fly from Dublin to Liverpool in a hot air balloon.[17]

After the first and second articles declaring popular sovereignty and the
right of resistance, the third read,

> III. Government is devised for the security of rights. The rights
> of man are liberty and an equal participation of the commonage of
> Nature.

The function of the state is to ensure equality in the commons. But what is
that? He elaborated somewhat this notion of "commonage." In the twenty-
sixth article he does this negatively by opposing the monopoly, hoarding, or
hogging of the earth, and incidentally suggests that the justification for such
imbalance may originate from the church or ancestors.

> XXVI. Those who believe that Heaven is, what earth has been, a
> monopoly in the hands of favored few, would do well to reconsider
> their opinion; if they find that it came from their priest or their grand-
> mother, they could not do better than reject it.

The twenty-eighth article connects the contradiction between wealth and
poverty.

> XXVIII. No man has a right to monopolize more than he can enjoy;
> what the rich give to the poor, whilst millions are starving, is not a
> perfect favor, but an imperfect right.

What do the Luddite's "commonality" and Shelley's "commonage" have
to do with each other besides coevality and etymology? They are not just
similar words from the same time: they refer to a human discussion of political economy and privatizing on one hand, and on the other, communism and
the commons.

Does communism belong to the field of politics while "the commons" belongs to the field of economics? Is communism a theory contrived by intellectuals and utopians while the practices of commoning are widespread, un-
lettered, and unrecognized? Certainly the Luddites combined both, a politics
of revolutionary insurrection with clear influences from the revolutionary
traditions of Ireland, France, and the 1790s, and a local defense of ancient

---

17. Richard Holmes, *The Age of Wonder: How the Romantic Generation Discovered the Beauty
and Terror of Science* (New York: Pantheon, 2008), 157, 162.

right and custom which were threatened by privatization, machinery, and enclosure. Is the commons just an aggregate sum to be arithmetically equally divided into aliquot parts? The view which presents the commons as a matter of equal social division is largely the idea of dreamers and intellectuals and as such it is scorned by cynics and realists. The idea certainly is found among the *philosophes* of the Enlightenment, such as, Rousseau, Mably, Morelly, or Volney.

The difference between Ludd's "commonality" and Shelley's "commonage" may be the difference between experience and aspiration. If so, in the England of the time the connection between them, tenuous though it was in 1811, was vigorously preserved by Thomas Spence. Spence, the London coiner of political tokens, the radical hymn singer, the pavement-chalker, and "unfee'd advocate of the disinherited seed of Adam," mixed the English strand of communism with "figurative descriptions of the Millenium, New Jerusalem, or future Golden Age." He appealed, like Shelley, to Volney's *Ruins*, and, unlike Shelley, to the Old Testament jubilee. If Shelley was often on the run, Spence was frequently imprisoned. Spence took inspiration from the mutineers of the Royal Navy in 1797, from the United Irish people in the rebellion of 1798, and from the resistance of indigenous people in America. His concept of true justice was based on equality in land the accomplishment of which constituted his "plan." He believed oppression could come to an end with some "rich Confiscations." Malcolm Chase calls Spence "one of the most sophisticated theoreticians of revolutionary radicalism," though his views could be extremely succinct: one of Spence's political coins summed them up, "War or Land."[18]

In 1811 a small society of Spenceans was formed in London, meeting on a neighborhood basis in the free and easy manner. Maurice Margarot returned to England from Australia whence he had been punitively transported in 1793 and joined the society. He also advocated "the Confiscation and Sale of all great estates." Attending the funeral of Thomas Spence in September 1814 was Robert Charles Fair who was converted to this cause of the commons by reading Shelley's *Queen Mab*. E.P. Thompson found it quite possible that Spencean disciples could be found among the strong and traveled characters of Yorkshire Luddites.

18. Malcolm Chase, *The People's Farm: English Radical Agrarianism, 1775–1840* (London: Breviary Stuff Publications, 2010), 46, 56, 59.

The views of another utopian socialist, we know, were definitely present in the discussions taking place in the cropper's shed. There George Mellor in 1812 heard the view of Robert Owen "that the whole framework of society was out of joint, and that the nations and governments of the earth required a thorough remodeling." The Luddites may have been hungry, pinched, and wretched; some may have clung stubbornly to the commons of a traditional, even a Tudor, economy; yet they were not out of touch with the intellectual work required of political change, or dismissive of the erudition that can help it. The argument that the nations and governments of the earth required re-modeling was advanced by a man whose father, also a cropper, kept a bed in the workshop where he sat up for many a night compiling a Greek lexicon![19] I'm not arguing that all Luddites studied utopian socialism or Greek, but some did, and others listened to them.

V.

In traveling in the north Shelley gained some experience of the poverty, exploitation, and military repression from which the people suffered. Extreme economic conditions and solidifying class identities were new in comparison to the 1790s. On Christmas Day 1811 he wrote William Godwin, whose *Political Justice*, he says, converted him from romance to reason, "I have been led into reasonings which make me *hate* and more the existing establishment of every kind." He anticipates the bursting of the storm when "the oppressed take furious vengeance on the oppressors."[20] "Shall I not get into Prison," he asked in a letter "that his Majesty will provide me a lodging in consideration of the zeal which I evince for the bettering of his subjects." Shelley began to plan a long poem eventually to become *Queen Mab* which he thought he might be able to publish in Dublin.

Before departing the north of England he wrote a factual, narrative poem, "A Tale of Society as It Is," about a widow whose son was pressed into the army,

> *For seven years did this poor woman live*
> *In unparticipated solitude.*

19. Peel, *Risings of the Luddites*, 14–15.
20. Holmes, *Shelley: The Pursuit* (New York: Dutton, 1975), 98.

Thou might have seen her in the desert rude
Picking the scattered remnants of its wood.
If human, thou might'st there have learned to grieve.

It's the theme found in also in Wordsworth's *Prelude* and one might think little had changed from then until 1939 when George Orwell observed the Moroccan women carrying wood thinking that they were of a different race entirely.[21] These men were passing through, and in not talking with the women they were unable to discover the custom of estovers. They do not see the commons; the commons is not a natural resource exclusive of human relations with it. Like language itself, the commons increases in wealth by use.

The colonial Atlantic begins a short balloon ride away. Shelley wrote *An Address to the Irish People*. "Oh! Ireland! Thou emerald of the ocean, whose sons are generous and brave, whose daughters are honorable and frank and fair, thou art the isle on whose green shores I have desired to see the standard of liberty erected—a flag of fire—a beacon at which the world shall light the torch of Freedom!" As he wrote, "I consider the State of Ireland as constituting a part of a great crisis in opinions." "It is horrible that the lower classes must waste their lives and liberty to furnish means for their oppressors to oppress them yet more terribly. It is horrible that the poor must give in taxes what would save them and their families from hunger and cold; it is still more horrible that they should do this to furnish further means of their own abjectness and misery."[22]

The title of the poem *Queen Mab* is significant. Shelley was a strong believer in the intervention of spirit in the history of the world (past and to come), and Queen Mab was such a spirit—a fairy, capable of flight, and the sender of dreams. In those warring, repressive, and hungry times Shelley made supernatural appeal. For another thing Mab had a powerful association with the earth. She was a major figure in Irish legend as Maeve (or Mebh) going back at least to the eighth and ninth centuries, a female warrior deity magically associated with the land.

In England Queen Mab was associated with the tiny, entomological world of leaves and soil before the earth had become a homogeneous rent-

21. George Orwell, "Marrakech" in *Essays*.
22. David Lee Clark (ed.), *Shelley's Prose; or, The Trumpet of a Prophecy* (Albuquerque: University of New Mexico Press, 1954), 108, 122.

making machine.[23] In America Charles Brockden Brown in his 1799 novel *Edgar Huntley* (a favorite of Shelley) named Queen Mab an ancient Delaware indigenous woman who intransigently refused to budge from her ancestral lands despite the overwhelming encroachment of the white settlers. Thus, Shelley's title appealed to the magical sublime of first, the colonial, second, the indigenous, and third, the agrarian. *Queen Mab* was a direct allusion to a power figure in Irish history at a time when Ireland had ceased to exist as a sovereign political entity and to the enchanted landscape of pre-enclosed England at a time of brutal privatization.

It was a communist poem in a mystical way because its grip on the actualities of the expropriation of the commons was occasional. To Thelwall's list of estates, rights and possessions of the poor enclosed by the rich, Shelley added another dimension. He sensed that the expropriations in England passing under the name of "improvement" and recognized by historians as "agrarian patriotism" were part of a worldwide devastation. "Rule of law" meant "freedom of contract" and "private property" in Nottinghamshire or elsewhere that English power went. For instance, when John Stamford Raffles invaded and governed Java in 1811 he introduced a system of money land rent which threatened the common rights of *sikep* villagers, discouraged cotton exports, and curtailed common rights in the teak forests, as well as fulfilling the prophecy of 1805, "the beginning of the ruin of the land of Java."[24]

VI.

No sooner had Shelley arrived in Ireland than he was reading in an American newspaper about Hidalgo and Morelos and the struggle the year before for Mexican independence. In "To the Republicans of North America" he wrote,

> *Brothers! Between you and me*
> *Whirlwinds sweep and billows roar:*
> *Yet in spirit oft I see*

23. See Mercutio's speech in *Romeo and Juliet*, I.iv.
24. Bayly, *Imperial Meridian*, 6, 14, 80, 121; Peter Carey, *The Power of Prophecy: Prince Dipanagara and the End of the Old Order in Java, 1785–1855* (Leiden: KITLV Press, 2007), 33, 179, 258.

On this wild and winding shore
Freedom's bloodless banners wave

He called on Cotopaxi, an Ecuadorean volcano, to act as the roaring tocsin of worldwide liberty and then for the waves and winds of the ocean to bear its news to Europe. Anna Laetitia Barbauld ended her poem *Eighteen Hundred and Eleven* by also attributing prophetic power to another Ecuadorean volcano, Chimborazo, bidding America to rise.

And rise America did, but not without struggle, only its enclosures were conquest of Indian lands and its Luddites were insurrectionary slaves. The destruction of farm implements by those working them on American plantations belongs to the story of Luddism, not just because they too were tool-breakers, but they were part of the Atlantic recomposition of textile labor-power. They grew the cotton that was spun and woven in Lancashire. The story of the plantation slaves has been separated from the story of the Luddites. Whether separation was owing to misleading distinctions between wage and slave labor or to artificial national or racial differences is unclear.

A South Carolina planter wrote in 1855, "The wear and tear of plantation tools is harassing to every planter who does not have a good mechanic at his nod and beck every day in the year. Our plows are broken, our hoes are lost, our harnesses need repairing, and large demands are made of the blacksmith, the carpenter, the tanner, and the harnessmaker." Eugene Genovese adds, "The implements used on the plantation were therefore generally much too heavy for efficient use. The "nigger hoe," often found in relatively advanced Virginia, weighed much more than the "Yankee hoe," which slaves broke easily. Those used in the southwest weighed almost three times as much as those manufactured in the North for Northern use." A Louisiana editor wrote in 1849, "They break and destroy more farming utensils, ruin more carts, break more gates, spoil more cattle and horses and commit more waste than five times the number of white laborers do."[25]

We are not used to such juxtapositions; economic history is generally conducted by presupposing general exchange value rather than particular use-value. Its language tends to be abstract. We consider "capital" or we consider "property" in our debates about Luddism, and behind them other abstractions

---

25. Eugene D. Genovese, *The Political Economy of Slavery: Studies in the Economy & Society of the Slave South* (New York: Vintage, 1967), 55; *Roll, Jordan, Roll: The World the Slaves Made* (New York: Pantheon, 1974), 300.

such as "technology" or "law." Yet these machines used or consumed cotton and wool, the one grown on the plantation, the other raised in the pastures. Who covered themselves with the woolen blankets? Who wore the cotton clothes? These are the questions of use-value. They lead the mind more easily to the human story and to the human struggle. The soldiers and the sailors wore the clothes, people in Latin America especially after 1808 used the blankets. There is a violence in abstraction which hides the negotiation of uses inherent in commoning.

The history of Louisiana between 1803 and 1812 is instructive. In the former year it was purchased by the United States; in the latter it became the eighteenth U.S. state. In each case slave rebellion preceded the change. Spain had ceded Louisiana to France in 1800, the same year that Thomas Jefferson was elected president and Gabriel Prosser led an ambitious revolt of Virginia slaves. Jefferson's policy was to civilize the wilderness, where "civilize" meant surveyed, saleable public lands—or the treatment of the earth as commodity and constant capital, and where "wilderness" meant the communal possession and use by the Choctaw, Chickasaw, and Creek people. His policy was both conquest and privatization. Moreover, he doubled the land area of the United States in 1803 by the purchase of Louisiana territories from Napoleon who used the money to finance a failed invasion of San Domingue and the reinstallation of the slave regime. The Louisiana Purchase provided the conditions for a dual economy of sugar in New Orleans and cotton from Georgia to Natchez, Mississippi, an economy based on the cotton gin (1793) and a surge of enslaved labor from Africa. These developments were fiercely resisted. As suggested in the archaeology of language where the settler qualified every plan with the expression "if the Creeks don't rise" similar to the devotional expression in-shalla.

The Creeks were divided between accommodationists and warriors. The accommodationists accepted the loom and the hoe as the technological entrance to a future of assimilation. The warriors were called Red Sticks led by Peter McQueen and Alexander McGillivray, inspired by the Shawnee warrior, Tecumseh, opposed the commerce and new forms of property, and destroyed the loom and bolts of cloth of accommodationists.[26]

26. Adam Rothman, *Slave Country: American Expansion and the Origins of the Deep South* (Cambridge, MA: Harvard University Press, 2005), 34–39.

Meanwhile, the slaves on the sugar plantations rose in revolt. An army of two to five hundred young men from Kongo, Cuba, Kentucky, Senegambia, Virginia, maroon and mulatto, assembled on a rainy night in January 1811 and marched down the Mississippi River to New Orleans determined to kill the whites and establish a black republic. Inspired by both Haiti and Hidalgo, this was the largest revolt of slaves in USA history. The "plantation tool [was] transmuted into an icon of violent insurrection," writes its historian. Armed with hoes, axes, and machetes they were totally outgunned and suffered a brutal massacre. More than a hundred bodies were dismembered and skulls displayed on poles up and down the Mississippi.[27] This took place in one of the richest commons of the world, the Mississippi River delta, which yet was the target of U.S. expansionism, as surveyors, missionaries, squatters, and the militia invaded.

"My soul has grown deep like the rivers," mourned Langston Hughes, the Afro-American poet of the underdog and common life. The indigenous people fought for a commons resisting the commodification of their mother Earth as real estate. The slaves rose against the plantation which from one point of view vied with Haiti in the export of sugar, and from another point of view was as near a death camp as could be imagined in the nineteenth century.

The results of the defeats of Creeks and slaves were twofold. First, the resistance of slaves and indigenous people was criminalized, and to accomplish this intensified applications of force—both a local militia and a federal military were relocated to the plantation south. Second, an alliance between federal authority and the state planters, between bureaucrats and slavocrats, was made whose militarization and racialization became pillars of the U.S. regime. In 1812 Louisiana became the eighteenth U.S. state. No defeat of the people's struggle is ever totally complete. The struggle continued in cultural forms from the delta blues of the 1930s to the *Pogo* comics of the 1950s, the swamps and bayous became the habitat of autonomous communities. These results had parallels among the Luddites of 1811–12. Cultural memory preserved a pantheon of mythological avatars of the history of the common people.

27. Daniel Rasmussen, *American Uprising: The Untold Story of America's Largest Slave Revolt* (New York: HarperCollins, 2011).

VII.

When Napoleon invaded Portugal and Spain in 1808 and installed his brother as king, the Spanish king fled, the empire began to crumble, and it lost its constitutional center, impelling a crisis between creoles and peninsulars in the Latin American colonies which became the context of the first wars of independence. Other class and ethnic forces found the opening to express their grievances and to fight for redress.

Francisco de Miranda, the Atlantic revolutionary, the "Precursor," left London and arrived in Caracas on December 10, 1811, bringing a pamphlet from Jeremy Bentham (*Constitutional Legislation: On the Evils of Change*), and formed the Patriotic Club open to men and women, blacks and Indians. English authorities in March 1811 continued to advise him, "nothing will become more important than the establishment of a regular and effective police for the protection of persons and property," wrote Vansittart, the chancellor of the exchequer, to Generalissimo Miranda.[28]

A rare version of the Venezuela flag showing a dark skinned man carrying a staff with the bonnet rouge. The cap of liberty signified manumission and equality.

In addition to the royalists and the creoles a third force emerged in Venezuela. On the one hand the *llaneros* of the south, a mixture of African, European, and Indian fighting to retain pastoral hunting, and on the other hand in the towns "the *pardos*, blacks and slaves fought for their own liberation." This was an "*insurrección de otra especie*," called the pardocracy, or government by the blacks and slaves. They participated in the "popular assemblies" and occasionally revolted independently as in June 1812. In November 1811 the *pardos* invaded the town council of Cartagena forcing it to sign a declaration of independence.[29] Bolívar's Cartagena Manifesto of December 1812 blamed the failure of this first republic upon

28. Karen Racine, *Francisco de Miranda: A Transatlantic Life in the Age of Revolution* (Wilmington, DE: Scholarly Resources, 2003), 216, 226, 232.
29. Marixa Lasso, *Myths of Harmony: Race and Republicanism during the Age of Revolution* (Pittsburgh: University of Pittsburgh Press, 2007), 1; John Lynch, *The Spanish American Revolutions, 1808–1826* (New York: Norton, 1973), 205.

"certain worthy visionaries who, conceiving in their minds some ethereal republic, have sought to attain political perfection, assuming the perfectibility
of the human race."[30] This was the spirit which Shelley expressed and which
led to his expulsion over and over again. In England the visionaries were
Godwin, Spence, Volney, and Shelley.

Perhaps too it was the spirit which is found among the Indians of Mexico
who in the Hidalgo revolt allied with the Virgin of Guadalupe. The Mexican War of Independence commenced on September 16, 1810, when Miguel
Hidalgo uttered the *grito de Dolores* and the Indians and mestizos mobilized
against the King and for the redistribution of land. Hidalgo was fiercely egalitarian having grown up with Indian workers on his father's land and speaking
several indigenous languages. He read Rousseau.[31] He encouraged the illegal
cultivation of olive groves and vine. His program of land reform was printed
on December 1810. It decreed the return of land *á las comunidades de los
naturales, para que enterándolas en la caja nacional, se entreguen á los referidos
naturales las tierras para su cultivo.* Hidalgo's army was large, and it took ad-
vantage of the *tumultos*, or riots, mutinies, and commotions which expressed
village goals, and it assaulted property including "the wanton destruction
of mining machinery."[32] These opposed encroachments on communal and
pueblo land by the market-driven haciendas; Oscar Lewis states, "The system of communal landholding has remained practically intact through both
the Aztec and Spanish conquests," and Brian Hamnett describes some of the
encroachments, "Villagers bitterly resented hacienda efforts to curb their
customary practices of chopping wood, burning charcoal, tapping maguey,
prickly pear, gathering wild lettuce, or grazing their few animals on lands
hitherto utilized by estate owners."[33] Hidalgo was defeated in 1811.

30. John Lynch, *Simón Bolívar: A Life* (New Haven: Yale University Press, 2006), 54, 56, 63, 68.
31. "A Provincial Library in Colonial Mexico, 1802," *Hispanic American Historical Review* 26,
no. 2 (May 1946), the library belonged to one of his associates in Guanajuato. Volney's *Ruins*
is not among the books listed.
32. Eric Van Young calls them "village soviets." See his *The Other Rebellion: Popular
Violence, Ideology, and the Mexican Struggle for Independence, 1810–1821* (Stanford: Stanford
University Press, 2001); and John Lynch, *The Spanish American Revolutions, 1808–1826* (New
York: Norton, 1973), 309.
33. Oscar Lewis, *Tepoztlán Village in Mexico* (New York: Holt, Rinehart and Winston,
1960), 27; and see also, Robert Redfield, *Tepoztlán: A Mexican Village: A Study of Folk Life*
(Chicago: University of Chicago Press, 1930), 62ff; Brian R. Hamnett, *Roots of Insurgency:
Mexican Regions, 1750–1824* (Cambridge: Cambridge University Press, 1986), 90.

VIII.

Tecumseh (1768–1813) confronted Governor Harrison in August 1810 with his famous speech about the commons when he said that the Indians considered "their lands as common property of the whole"—the basis of confederation. Denouncing land cessions, he exclaimed to Governor Harrison in Indiana, "Sell a country! Why not sell the air, the great sea, as well as the earth? Did not the Great Spirit make them all for the use of his children?" When Harrison, the future president, said that the claim was "preposterous" Tecumseh rose in a flash of temper from the ground, (Indians preferred to sit on the ground, or as Tecumseh explained, "to repose on the bosom of their mother") and the future president drew his sword. Blood was not spilt that day, but the line had once again been drawn between native American commoning, and Euro-American privatizing. The association of indigenous American practices and the development of European ideas of communism go back at least to Thomas More's *Uto-pia* (1516). Was America a new world or was it, as the Greek etymology of "uto-pia" suggests, a "no place" similar to the *terra nullius* of legal Latin lingo.

Tecumseh, by Benson J. Lossing, 1869

A year later in 1811 Tecumseh's brother, Tenskatawa, or the Prophet, was defeated at the Battle of Tippeca-noe and the granaries destroyed.[34] After this atrocity Tecumseh went on a three-thousand-mile, six-month journey to the south. There expropriation occurred by means of money as credit and debt became the leverage of land losses. In October 1811 he delivered a war speech to the Muskogee in his attempt to renew a federation of the indigenous people against their destruction. Te-cumseh's speech was described by a fourteen-year-old, John Hunter, "such language, such gestures, and such feeling and fullness of soul contending for utterance, were exhibited by this untutored native of the forest in the central

---

34. Tenskatawa blamed the defeat on his menstruating wife who contaminated the ceremonies before the battle. John Sugden, *Tecumseh: A Life* (New York: Henry Holt, 1997), 257.

wilds of America, as no audience, I am persuaded, either in ancient or modern times ever before witnessed."

Hunter lived with the Osage until he was nineteen in 1816. Later he published his memoirs with its appetizing description of prolific commons. "The squaws raise for the consumption of their families, corn, tobacco, pumpkins, squashes, melons, gourds, beans, peas, and, with a few years past, potatoes in small quantities. They collect hazel nuts, hickory nuts, walnuts, chestnuts, pecan nuts, grass, or ground nuts, various kinds of acorns, wild liquorice, sweet myrrh, or anise root, and Pash-e-quak, a large bulbous root somewhat resembling the sweet potato in form, and very similar to the chestnut in flavour, though more juicy." "They also collect, in their seasons, crab and may apples, Osage oranges, three or four kinds of plums, strawberries, gooseberries, whortleberries, black and dew-berries, and a great variety of grapes."

The economy of these resources is described too. "All their various products, as well as those of the chase, are, in general, distributed in proportion to the members of each family concerned in their acquirement; though sometimes no distribution takes place, but all draw, as they want, from the supplying source, as a common reservoir, till it is exhausted." "Whenever a scarcity prevails, they reciprocally lend, or rather share with each other, their respective stores, till they are all exhausted. When the case is otherwise, the wants of such individuals are regarded with comparative indifference; though their families share in the stock, become otherwise common from the public exigency."[35]

These then were the major eruptions in America at the time of Ned Ludd. Not all had equal participation in the commonage of nature, though those without it were fighting to *attain* it as surely as those in England with some access to the commonality were fighting to *retain* it.

IX.

While E.P. Thompson's indispensable chapter on the Luddites stresses the Irish in Lancashire it otherwise rigorously keeps the focus upon the English context with two rhetorical exceptions when he compares their clandestine organization to extra-English, non-Anglo themes. Once it is to

35. John D. Hunter, *Memoirs of a Captivity Among the Indians of North America* (London: Longman, Hurst, Rees, Orme, and Brown, 1824), 257–58.

America (the authorities "were more powerless to uncover trade union lodges than Pizzarro's freebooters were to uncover golden chalices in the villages of Peru") and once to Wales ("there is a tract of secret history, buried like the Great Plain of Gwaelod beneath the sea.").[36] This secret history, he says, necessitates on the part of the historian some "constructive speculation." His figures of speech can help us if we treat them not as figures but suggestions, because they enable us to expand the range by adding to the insular lens an Atlantic optic. What was quietly underground in one part of the world may erupt in fury in another part. We have begun to do this with America. Now, Wales.

The Plain of Gwaelod is subterranean, lying beneath the shallow seas in the Bay of Cardigan, north Wales. According to Welsh legend, as modified by Thomas Love Peacock's novel the *Misfortunes of Elphin* (1829) once upon a time in the sixth century the plain consisted of extensive, fertile, level land which provided prosperity to the Welsh kingdom of the day, and attracted traders from as far away as Phoenica and Carthage. The people built an embankment to protect the land from tide and sea, but the watchman one night fell asleep drunk and the sea overran the plain which thereafter remained, like Atlantis, a source of mythic past prosperity if not an actual Golden Age, but not before the Welsh bards had carried its wisdom to King Arthur at Avalon.

Shelley was part of something similar, for an extensive reclamation project by building a new embankment in the estuary near Portmadoc. Large numbers of laborers were mobilized. Shelley, back from Ireland, was searching for a new place to set up his commune and found one at Tan-yr-allt not far from Tremadoc. It was not long before he became involved with the project leader and the hundreds workers whose cooperative labors were constructing such extensive infrastructure. The natural conditions of labor were dangerous and so too were its social conditions.

Shelley explained this in one of the prose notes to *Queen Mab* in which he argues in favor of vegetarianism by showing that the cultivation of meat a) requires far more land than the growing of grain and garden produce, and b) that cattle, sheep, and stock raising always entails commerce and is thus, in the long sweep of history, a source of aristocracy which is built on the ruin of "all that is good in chivalry and republicanism." Lasting happiness is unobtainable as long as incentives to avarice and ambition are available

36. Thompson, *The Making of the English Working Class*, 487, 497.

to the few. "The use of animal flesh and fermented liquors directly militates with this equality of the rights of man." Surplus labor could be removed only with a sober, subsistence economy. At this point Shelley provides a footnote within the footnote.

> It has come under the author's experience that some of the workmen on an embankment in North Wales, who, in consequence of the inability of the proprietor to pay them, seldom received their wages, have supported large families by cultivating small spots of sterile ground by moonlight.

The resort to commoning was in default of wages and occurred upon sterile ground at Portmadoc where "one of the most advanced community and commercial experiments of the period" was taking place.[37] Shelley antagonized the local landlord, a Tory and an aristocrat with estates in Ireland who organized and disciplined the labor, a man named Leeson. An assassin attempted to take Shelley's life. Perhaps with Home Office connivance Leeson or his agent arranged the attack which happened a few months before the January 1813 execution of fourteen Yorkshire Luddites. Shelley sought safety in Killarney Lakes, back in Ireland. As a class renegade throwing his lot with the commonality, he was not cowardly. In Wales meanwhile an Englishman in 1815 attempted to develop land south of Portmadoc as a hunting estate for visiting gentry but Welsh rural people violently resisted and the unenclosed common on Mynydd Bach whose open pasture and stands of conifer and copses of oak and beech persisted into the twentieth century.[38]

Queen Mab, conceived in 1811, privately published 1813, and frequently pirated thereafter, became the Bible of the working class for the next two generations. Its targets were organized religion, political tyranny, war, commerce, marriage, and prostitution. "*Queen Mab* is no less than an attempt to state the basis for an entire philosophy of life, an active and militant view of man confronting his society and his universe." Like T.S. Eliot's *The Waste Land*, the poem is fenced in with footnotes though *Queen Mab*'s are about, we might say, the commons rather than the waste. It contains six prose essays: on the labor theory of value, on necessity in the moral and material universe, on atheism, on Christianity, on free love and vegetarianism. Like the political

37. Holmes, *Shelley: The Pursuit*, 164.
38. Anne Kelly Knowles, *Calvinists Incorporated: Welsh Immigrants on Ohio's Industrial Frontier* (Chicago: University of Chicago Press, 1997), 95.

economists he accepts the labor theory of value, "There is no real wealth but the labour of man," though unlike the political economist he did not reckon either wealth or labor numerically or financially.

Queen Mab recuperates the radical discussions of the 1790s with heavy influence from William Godwin's theoretical anarchism and Constantin Volney's eloquent fable of the destruction of the commons in human history. With Godwin he finds that the tyrannical principle of power permeates all institutions. With Volney he finds that the human past contains within it the potential of fulfillment of the dream of liberté, égalité, and fraternité.

> *Let the axe*
> *Strike at the root, the poison-tree will fall.*

War is the business of kings and priests and statesmen. They conceal their selfishness with three words, God, Hell, and Heaven. To Shelley the machine encouraged slavishness:

> *Power, like a desolating pestilence,*
> *Pollutes whate'er it touches; and obedience*
> *Bane of all genius, virtue, freedom, truth,*
> *Makes slaves of men, and, of the human frame,*
> *A mechanized automaton. (iii, 175–180)*

Slavery and the machine produce the person as automaton. Maxine Berg, a contemporary historian of technological change, finds that historians have been reluctant to explore the relation between Luddism and the intellectual disputes over technological change, despite the fact, we might add, that the most brilliant political economist of the day, David Ricardo, changed his mind about machinery between the first publication in 1817 of *On Principles of Political Economy and Taxation* and its third edition in 1821 agreeing that it is "often very injurious to the interests of the class of labourers."[39]

To Shelley the machine is far from being a substitute for labor, the machine was a model for what the labor was to become.

> *A task of cold and brutal drudgery;*
> *Hardened to hope, insensible to fear,*
> *Scarce living pulleys of a dead machine,*

---

39. Maxine Berg, *The Machinery Question and the Making of Political Economy* (Cambridge: Cambridge University Press, 1980), 15.

Meer wheels of work and articles of trade
That grace the proud and noisy pomp of wealth! (v, 74–79)

Priests, kings, and statesmen desolate society with war, sophistry, and commerce. These translated easily into the triplets of Martin Luther King, Jr., or the demons of Milton. "The sordid lust of self" prevailed, "All things are sold," wrote Shelley. He anticipates a day when poverty and wealth, disease, war, and fame shall pass and Man shall stand among the creatures as "An equal amidst equals": woman and man equal and free: palaces ruins: prisons children's playgrounds. "Learn to make others happy," he advised. Shelley also takes the commodity form of wealth and says that trade or commerce ("the propensity to truck, barter, and exchange") is not inherent in human nature. The commons appears as universal benevolence or human virtue.

A brighter morn awaits the human day,
When every transfer of earth's natural gifts
Shall be a commerce of good words and works;
When poverty and wealth, the thirst of fame,
The fear of infamy, disease and woe,
War with its million horrors, and fierce hell
Shall live but in the memory of Time. (v, 251ff)

X.

I have placed the beginning of the Luddite risings of two hundred years ago in a worldwide perspective by referring to capitalist incursions at the same time upon traditional practices of commoning in Ireland, North Africa, South America, the Caribbean, and North America. Indonesia or India could be added. Certainly, the expropriations were resisted with the means at hand which included the tools of production. The redressers who were thus expropriated came to constitute, ideally if anachronistically, an *international* proletariat. This is most clear when considering the international textile industry, for its global division of labor propelled class developments from the cotton plantation to the Lancashire factory, but it is also true of the division of labor in the international food economy which increasingly relied on sugar. The real connections which paralleled the ideal ones occurred at sea. The proletariat from the expropriated commons of the world had an actual existence in the seafaring communities of the world's ports, hence we call it, without anachronism, the *terraqueous* proletariat. What was to prevent its revolutionary actualization for they surely were aware of the many roads not taken? An answer was provided by the Ratcliffe Highway murders which initiated processes of terror, xenophobia, and criminalization.

The Ratcliffe Highway Murders took place on the nights of December 7

W.H. Pyne's Microcosm (1814), is in the picturesque style and prettyfies dangerous or oppressive processes of labor, in this case dock work. Not yet mechanized, the work remains based on handicraft with its attendant interactions.

and 19, 1811. The servant of the Marrs family had been sent out to buy oysters for a late Saturday night dinner and returned having to knock repeatedly at the door, the first sign that a homicidal extermination had taken place in the linen-draper's house. Marr, his wife, their infant, and an apprentice had been brutally murdered by means of a maul and a ships carpenter's chisel. No property was taken. Less than two weeks later around the corner on New Gravel Lane in the same docker's neighborhood of Wapping, Mr. and Mrs. Williamson and a maid-servant were similarly bloodily murdered.[40]

A terrifying frenzy became intense and extensive. The "passionate enthusiasm" of the crowd, a "frenzied movement of mixed horror and exaltation," "a sublime sort of magnetic contagion," spread through the metropolis and the

40. T.A. Critchley and P.D. James, *The Maul and the Pear Tree: The Ratcliffe Highway Murders, 1811* (London: Constable, 1971).

country. Shelley in the Lake District must have known of it because he was in dialogue there with Robert Southey who wrote from Keswick, three hundred miles away, that the murder mingled horror and insecurity. It brought a stigma "on the land we live in." "The national character is disgraced." We shall see that it became a moment of chauvinism.

Among the many reactions I'd like to consider two essays by Thomas de Quincey, "On Murder as Considered One of the Fine Arts" and "The Knocking at the Gate in *Macbeth*," because they lead us to the major themes of modern life, despite their obscure perversity. He writes of the murderer, "there must be raging some great storm of passion,—jealousy, ambition, vengeance, hatred,—which will create a hell within him; and into this hell we are to look." Assuredly, we accept that this is true, that the individual was in a grip of a great storm of passion. Yet, the power of this individual passion can be best understood if we see that it is aligned with powerful *social* forces that were specific to the economics of the location. Hell was both within and without, subjective and social. De Quincey's second essay refers to a rare moment in Shakespearean tragedy when an important experience is represented by a low character providing the view from below.

The action at the beginning of Act II, scene iii, had reached a pitch of terror and tension in the murder of Duncan, when the knocking begins at the gate. To de Quincey, the porter's speech in *Macbeth* represents "the re-establishment of the goings-on of the world." The murder is insulated from "the ordinary tide and succession of human affairs." The knocking at the gate returns us to "the world of ordinary life." But it doesn't do this, or if it does it returns us to specifically *English* ordinary life. What the porter's speech actually reveals are several of the permanent antagonisms of English modernity, the moral economy and the criminalized wage, which for centuries were either ignored totally or expressed in slang, low speech, or cant. Let us look more closely.

The porter, hung over and slowly making his way to the door, mutters and compares himself to the porter of hell, not the homicidal introspective hell but a working-class, cynical hell damning it all. He doesn't have time to let in "all professions that go the primrose way to the everlasting bonfire," but two must be mentioned.

> Knock, knock, knock! Who's there in the name of Beelzebub? Here's
> a farmer that hanged himself on the expectation of plenty: come in
> time; have napkins enough about you; here you'll sweat for't.

This is a reference to the disappearing of the moral economy of the time,
c. 1606–7, as well as 1812 when in April Hannah Smith, fifty-four years old,
overturned a cart of potatoes in Manchester at the end of several days of a
food rioting. The cavalry suppressed the people and she was apprehended
for "highway robbery," nevertheless the prices of potatoes, butter, and milk
came down. She was hanged in May 1812. A casualty to the "moral economy"
whose complex market regulations expressed the ancient theme that none
should profit at the expense of another's want.[41]

> Knock, knock, knock! Who's there? Faith, here's an old English tai-
> lor come hither for stealing out of a French hose: come in, tailor; here
> you may roast your goose.

Before electricity the smoothing iron, called the "goose," was kept on a
fire. The reference is to the criminalization of the tailor's perquisites in the
remnants of the cloth he cut called cabbage and stored in the "taylor's reposi-
tory for his stolen goods" whose cant term was "Hell."[42] If the porter's view
of life is "ordinary," this ordinary life is hell.

The "hell" within the murderer is also the "hell" of criminalized customs
of the docks. For twenty years powerful commercial interests from Caribbean sugar planters to London ship owners, from Thames warehousemen
to the West India interest, worked with the Home Office to devise means to
destroy the customary compensation which the sailors, lumpers, and dock-
workers enjoyed as customs in common. John Herriott wrote, "we succeeded
by our joint efforts in bringing into reasonable order some thousands of men
who had long considered plunder as a privilege." The slippage from custom
to perquisite to privilege to plunder was the slide along the slippery slope of
criminalization. The coalheaver took two or three bushels of coal. "Custom
was their invariable plea," wrote Herriott.[43] Of the lumpers who unloaded

41. John Bohstedt, *Riots and Community Politics in England and Wales, 1790–1810*
(Cambridge: Harvard University Press, 1983), 162.
42. Francis Grose, *A Classical Dictionary of the Vulgar Tongue* (1796), edited by Eric
Partridge (New York: Barnes & Noble, 1963), 184.
43. John Herriott, *Struggles through Life*, 2 vols. (Philadelphia, 1809), ii, 260.

the West India vessels one witness testified to Parliament, "they could not subsist without (what they are pleased to Term) Perquisites."[44] A Parliamentary committee of 1823 asked a ship owner, "Therefore, this, which used to be called plunderage, was at least in a considerable degree, a mode of paying wages?" and the ship owner replied, "It was certainly an understood thing."[45]

They lived in a dockside community where subsistence depended on such customs. Patrick Colquhoun labeled them "crime," convincing the propertied public and Parliament as well. This was an upside-down world Shelley described where opulence and luxury of the few were purchased by the disease, penury, and crime of the many. "The worm is in thy core," wrote Anna Barbauld, "Crime walks thy streets, Fraud earns her unblest bread." The density of habitation, collective living arrangements, inns, boarding houses, pawn shops, slop shops, second hand shops, old iron shops, receiving kens, fences, brothels, constituted an urban economic structure of opacity which Patrick Colquhoun was determined to destroy.

Two policies were followed to accomplish this end. William Tatham, a political economist of inland navigation, contrasted the care given to the *centrifugal* tendencies of overseas commerce with the neglect of *centripetal* facilities of the amazing transfer of unbounded wealth.[46] In other words England's strength in its navy contrasted with weakness in its police. Police could not easily be introduced as it had to overcome more than a century's opposition after the experience of Oliver Cromwell's military dictatorship and the consequent hostility to a standing army. Furthermore police were associated with France, the national enemy, and French dictatorship. Thus the introduction of a police force into England had to be protracted beginning at the end of the eighteenth century with small or niche forces (Bow Street patrol, Thames River police) and broadening from Irish police experience in the early nineteenth century into England. Peel's Peace Preservation Act of 1814, a police act, the result of the property panic after the Ratcliffe Highway murders, was another such step. The second policy against the underground economy of the waterfront was an investment of constant capital in dockside infrastructure, colossal building projects accomplished in the first decade of the century which at once destroyed dockers' neighborhoods and created ti-

44. *Parliamentary Papers*, vol. 17 (1795–1796), xxvi.
45. *Parliamentary Papers*, vol. 4, 225.
46. William Tatham, *The Political Economy of Inland Navigation* (London, 1799), 133.

tantic enclosures of walls, locks, and canals. In fact, the first Ratcliffe Highway murders occurred across the road from such a commercial fortress.

XI.

Conventional historiography, even labor history, has not included these struggles which are still stigmatized by the discourse of criminality, or DeQuincy's "world of ordinary life." Over ten years beginning in 1803 "almost the entire paternalist code was swept away."[47] The regulations regarding the woolen trade were suspended and then in 1809 repealed. In 1813 the apprenticeship clauses of 5 Eliz. I c.4 were repealed. The clauses which had permitted magistrates to set minimum wages were abolished. During the same period the last common law means of price-fixing were destroyed and laws against forestalling and regrating (two forms of profiteering—keeping goods from sale, buying in order to sell respectively) were not renewed.

The forces of order looked for a kind of catharsis to purge the property holders of their fears. The murders produced a firestorm of chauvinism: Germans, Danes, Indians, Portuguese, and finally Irish were suspected, and a roundup of forty to fifty people quickly ensued.

John Williams, a sailor who had been discharged two months earlier in October 1811, widely believed to have been Irishman from co. Down was apprehended. Williams lodged at the Pear Tree in Old Wapping. He had once sailed with Marr and with William Ablass, a.k.a. "Long Billy," born in Danzig. They sailed from Rio de Janeiro to Demarara, Surinam, where the crew mutinied. John Williams was committed to Cold Bath Fields and widely believed to have been scapegoated.[48]

Divine Service on Christmas Day in Greenwich was interrupted by the alarm drum beating to arms. River fencibles (soldiers liable for defensive service only) repaired to their post to do their duty. Was it another assassin or had the French invaded? A large party of Irish had been drinking and fell into faction fighting. People were afraid to go out of doors. Five hundred

47. Thompson, *The Making of the English Working Class* (London: Gollancz, 1963), 544.
48. Critchley and James, *The Maul and the Pear Tree*, 174: "the key questions still unanswered" and Leon Radzinowicz, *A History of English Criminal Law and Its Administration*, volume iii, *The Reform of the Police* (London: Stevens, 1956), 322: "He was, without doubt, the murderer . . ."

Shadwell householders met on Christmas Day to arm themselves and form volunteer associations.

John Williams was found dead in his prison, an apparent suicide. His body delivered to Shadwell magistrates who, with approval of the Home Office, mounted it on a cart, in full open display, and paraded it on New Year's Eve in the neighborhood in front of ten thousand people before driving a stake through its heart beneath the paving stones of Old Gravel Lane, a "salutary example to the lower orders." The corpse of the sailor, John Williams, was subject to public, theatrical, and ritualized humiliation. It was a savage moment in the history of English law comparable to the dismemberment and humiliation in 1806 of Jean-Jacques Dessalines, the black ruler of Haiti. Richard Ryder was the Home Secretary, a reactionary and feeble man. Like Spencer Perceval, the Prime Minister, who always wore black, Ryder was an evangelical.

Richard Brinsley Sheridan, the Irish playwright and member of Parliament, said "they fed the worst appetites of the mob in the unseemly exhibition of the dead body to the multitude." In the midst of public hysteria the prime minister, Perceval, spoke admitting frankly that the murders were not solved and joined the clamor for more police. He was assassinated on May 11, 1812. Sheridan spoke out against English xenophobia. "The prejudice of the hour would have him an Irishman." They were made to cross themselves as corroboration. "It was nothing but an Irish murder and could have been done only by Irishmen! Beastly as this prejudice was, the Shadwell magistrates were not ashamed to act up to it in all the meanness and bigotry of its indignant spirit, viewing the murder in no less a light than that of a Popish plot."

The murders were quickly brought within a counterrevolutionary agenda. *The Newgate Calendar* conjectured that he was a veteran of the 1798 rebellion. "In the dreadful paths of rebellion probably it was that he was first tempted to imbrew his hands in the blood of his fellow creatures," and its terrible scenes of midnight murder."[49] Modern historians of the murder call Williams' arrest "a blatant example of racialism and anti-Catholicism."[50] A letter to the Hunts' *The Examiner* (Jan 9, 1812) expressed the view that "to keep the natives of

49. During the Parliamentary debate on the police, Cochrane ascribed increase in crimes to "the Pension List and to the various other modes by which individuals of the higher classes . . . partook of the public money, without performing any public service" which demoralized the lower classes and drove them to the commission of offences. 336.
50. Critchley and James, *The Maul and the Pear Tree*, 200.

Ireland ignorant and barbarous at home and to calumniate them to the rest of Europe was the object of every succeeding chief governor of that country." More was involved. The terraqueous humanity of the East End of the London docks was further terrorized and divided by religion, by ethnicity, by property, by country of origin.

The procession was led by the constable, the collector of taxes, a coal merchant, and the "superintendant of Lascars in the East India Company's service." This was rough street theatre of nationalism and class discipline. Lascars comprised 60 percent of the merchant service in 1814. They were seamen hired in Bengal to sail East India ships back to Britain. They were often kidnapped, mistreated on the six months voyage, paid between one sixth and one seventh the rate of the European sailor, and abandoned naked, cold, and destitute once the ship arrived on the Thames and delivered of its cargo. One thousand four hundred and three Lascars arrived in 1810, and one hundred died within the year. A missionary sent among them in 1813 declared them "senseless worshippers of dumb idols" and "practically and abominably wicked." There was a depot for them on Ratcliffe Highway where they were overcrowded, underfed, and often punished. The East India Company's medical attendant said such reports came only "from the discontented and criminal."[51] And yet it was entirely likely that such a lascar provided Thomas Spence with his knowledge of Buddhism which he printed in *The Giant Killer*, the newspaper he had begun to publish just before his death in 1814.

Wapping imports as well as the commodities of empire—its "goods" to use the hypocritical term—also the people, and sometimes, like the crew of the *Roxburgh Castle*, according to Captain Hutchinson they could be "very bad."[52] Williams enlisted on the East Indiaman, *Roxburgh Castle*, bound to the Brazils, in August 1810 and fourteen months later discharged in Wapping. Detained a long time at Rio where the captain warned Williams that if he ever were to go on land he was bound to be hanged. The ship then proceeded to Demerara, where the crew mutinied, to be put down by Captain Kennedy of the naval brig *Forester*. He had been in Rio de Janeiro aboard the ship

51. Rozina Visram, *Ayahs, Lascars and Princes: Indians in Britain 1700–1947* (London: Pluto Press, 1986), 34, 39, and 45. In 1806 Chinese and lascar sailors erupted in riot in Ratcliffe Gardens when the captain of their ship ordered a lascar to flog a Chinese sailor. I am grateful to Iona Man-Cheong and her paper, "Chinese Seafarers & Acts of Resistance in the 'Age of Revolution,'" Mutiny and Maritime Radicalism, Amsterdam, (June 2011).
52. *The Times*, January 1, 1812, 166.

Roxburgh Castle at a time when the royal Navy was actively exploiting the opening left by the collapse of the Spanish empire and in patrolling ships to enforce the ban on the slave trade. Captain Kennedy was a severe officer who wielded the lash with exceptional enthusiasm.[53] Three mutinous sailors were confined in Surinam, including William Ablass, a.k.a. "Long Billy," a leader of the mutiny, and drinking partner of Williams in Wapping.

The English had taken over the colony from the Dutch in 1803 and by 1811 sugar was replacing cotton and coffee as the export crop and John Gladstone was establishing his enormous interests. Guyanese slaves had shifted 100 million tons of earth with their long-handled shovels creating what the Dutch called *polders*, or land reclaimed from the sea, and what Walter Rodney called "a tremendous contribution to the *humaniʒation* of the Guyanese coastal landscape." With sugar came steam powered mills which "saved" labor in the mill and intensified it in the fields. Hence, more slaves.

With steam and slavery came spiritual uplift whose mind-forged manacles were forged in mandatory chapel. In 1810 a law was passed against obeah, an Afro-Caribbean religious practice criminalized as witchcraft or sorcery. In 1811 John Wray, the missionary, wrote a Christian catechism of obedience, and against theft, waste, and negligence, which parallels the repressive injunctions of Patrick Colquhoun and John Herriot against customary takings on the river Thames. In the same year the government issued regulations for religious instruction (registration of instructors, location of chapels, noninterference with hours of toil, confinement to estate, etc.) which when reissued in 1823 helped to spark the great slave rebellion.[54] In 1811 Carmichael, the English governor, made English the language of rule and named the principle town for the new regent, Georgetown, as that was the year George III was declared irrevocably mad and the regency begun. In Trinidad that year it was prophesied that before long "white men will be burning in hell."[55]

The movement to village autonomy that began after the slave revolts of 1823 produced a democratic, proud community of ex-slaves which the London *Times* was to call "little bands of Socialists."[56] Machine-breaking was not

53. I owe this knowledge to Niklas Frykman, who studied Captain Kennedy's log for 1811.
54. Emilia Viotti da Costa, *Crowns of Glory, Tears of Blood: The Demerara Slave Rebellion of 1823* (New York: Oxford University Press, 1994), 40, 99, 111, 175.
55. Richard Watson, *A Defence of the Wesleyan Methodist Mission in the West Indies* (1817), 75.
56. As quoted in Walter Rodney, *A History of Guyanese Working People, 1881–1905* (Baltimore: Johns Hopkins University Press, 1981), 128.

unknown. Ken Robertson, my fellow worker in Toledo, Ohio, tells the story of Mr. Samuels who lost his hand to a mechanical coconut shredder and in response four men from his twin village, Golden Grove and Nabaclis, "set fire to the pumping station in the wee small hours of one wretched unforgettable morning."[57]

XII.

It was the sailors of the world who manned the most expensive of machines, the deep-water sailing ship. Commerce and globalization depended on them. They mutinied and were notoriously answered with terror. John Williams was confined within the same cells of Cold Bath Fields prison that fifteen years earlier had held the mutineers of the Nore whose red flag, "floating republic," and direct action were inspirational to Thomas Spence, Walt Whitman, and Herman Melville as well as to innumerable sailors as far away as Cape of Good Hope or Bengal.[58] A few short years after the mutiny William Wordsworth, in the preface (1802) to *Lyrical Ballads* wrote, "the Poet binds together by passion and knowledge the vast empire of human society as it is spread over the whole earth, and over all time," forgetting to add that, howsoever such binding may take place (what passions? whose knowledge?), it could not be done without the sailor.

Hell is an element that recurs. Not long after the assassination of Perceval in May 1812 Ryder, still home secretary, received this letter from Manchester Luddites (without benefit of spell-check),[59]

> Theirfore you may Prepaire to go to the Divel to Bee Secraterry for Mr Perceval theire for there are fire Ships Making to saile by land as well as by Warter that will not faile to Destroy all the Obnoctious in the both Houses as you have been a great Deal of pains to Destroy

57. Kenneth Joyce Robertson, *The Four Pillars: A Genealogical Journey* (Xlibris, 2010), 160. A remarkable book of valuable inventories, archival labor, and pointed anecdote written by a Guyanese market fruit-juicer of Toledo who traces his ancestry to Ignatius Sancho, the grocer and man of letters of eighteenth-century London.
58. Michael Fisher, "Finding Lascar 'Wilful Incendiarism': British Arson Panic and Indian Maritime Labor in the Indian and Atlantic Oceans" and Nicole Ulrich, "Local Protest and International Radicalism: the 1797 Mutinies at the Cape of Good Hope," Mutiny and Maritime Radicalism during the Age of Revolution, Amsterdam (June 2011).
59. Binfield, *Writings of the Luddites*, 1.

Chiefe part of the Country it is know your turn to fall. The Remedy
for you is Shor Destruction Without Detection—prepaire for thy
Departure and Recommend the same to thy friends
Your Hble sert &c
Luddites

Thus, from Blake's satanic mills to the Luddite's damnation of the prime
minister and home secretary, from Shakespeare's porter to Milton's demons,
from Shelley's hell of war to de Quincy's hell of murder, the material struc-
tures of modern English history—commercial agriculture, enclosures, the
criminalized artisan, the factory, and the machine—were likened to the place
of burning fires and eternal torment.

Queen Mab does not belong to that infernal tradition. The widening gulf
between rich and poor is deplored and denounced in language of both ten-
derness and wrath that does not rely on the myths of the Inferno. Influenced
by Godwin and Volney, Shelley nevertheless appeals to a metaphysics of his
own which owes something to local, folk, and nonmonotheistic spirits. Inas-
much as hell is underground the two traditions overlap with the Ecuadorean
volcanoes, the Mississippi valley earthquake, the plain of Gwaelod, and the
coalmines.

The application of steam power required extraction of coal by digging
more deeply which the steam engine also enabled. The miner is described in
Queen Mab.

> . . . *yon squalid form,*
> *Leaner than fleshless misery, that wastes*
> *A sunless life in the unwholesome mine,*
> *Drags out in labour a protracted death*
> *To glut their grandeur. (iii, 12ff)*

On May 24, 1812, in Sunderland took place the great Felling colliery disaster when ninety-two were killed, twenty younger than fourteen and one
boy eight years old. This inspired Davy's invention of the safety lamp whose
construction he brilliantly described in an inexpensive publication, "with
the hope of presenting a permanent record of this important subject to the
practical miner, and of enabling the friends of humanity to estimate and apply those resources of science, by which a great and permanently existing

evil may be subdued."[60] Humphrey Davy had lectured to packed theatres in Dublin the year before; in 1812 William Godwin took has fourteen-year-old daughter, Mary, to listen to Davy lecture in London.[61] In *Frankenstein* (1817) Mary depicts the monster pathetically listening outside the window of a lonely mountain cottage to a peasant family reading aloud Volney's *Ruins* and how it came to be that the commons was lost and mankind was divided between rich and poor. The hunted subaltern product of scientific progress cocks his ear to the social effects of economic development, enclosure and class separation, or X^2.

In *Queen Mab* Shelley expresses the philosophy of Necessitarianism, a doctrine of the powerful. "History, politics, morals, criticism, all grounds of reasonings, all principles of science, alike assume the truth of the doctrine of Necessity." These are the assumptions of power, inevitability, necessity, fate. Shelley continues, "No farmer carrying his corn to market doubts the sale of it at the market price. The master of a manufactory no more doubts that he can produce the human labor necessary of his purposes than his machinery will act as they have been accustomed to act." Shelley is conscious of convulsive events in Manchester, and alludes to both permanent antagonisms of modernity, the moral economy and Luddism. He was not a determinist or a fatalist, and nor were the Luddites.

Looking back two hundred years from the vantage point of 2011 it is easier to see that the proletariat was not insular or particular to England. It had suffered traumatic loss as we have seen in a few of the myriad commons of 1811 such as the Irish knowledge commons, the agrarian commons of the Nile, the open fields of England enclosed by Acts of Parliament, the Mississippi delta commons, the Creek-Chickasaw-Cherokee commons, the *llaneros* and *pardos* of Venezuela, the Mexican *comunidades de los naturales*, the eloquently expressed nut-and-berry commons of the Great Lakes, the customs of the *sikep* villagers of Java, the subsistence commons of Welsh gardeners, the commons of the street along the urban waterfront, the lascars crammed in dark spaces far from home, and the Guyanese slaves building commons and community—and these losses were accomplished by terrifying machines—the man-

---

60. Humphry Davy, *On the Fire-Damp in Coal Mines and on Methods of Lighting the Mines So As to Prevent Explosion* (Newcastle: E. Charnley, 1817).
61. Holmes, *The Age of Wonder*, 304, 325.

of-war, the steam engine, the cotton gin—which therefore were not seen as "improvement," "development," or "progress" but as hell itself.

The steam engine of Lancashire in 1811–12 differed from the steam engine of Fukushima of 2011 in the source of power. But otherwise, is Fukushima but a scaling up of the machine opposed by the Luddites? Of course not, because hammers would not bring redress, only radioactive contamination. Yet, the technologies and science of both machines were products of war in the nineteenth and twentieth centuries respectively. They both have "augmented the general inquietude of man," to quote John Charnock, an engineer of the men-of-war of the Napoleonic period.[62] He referred to these engines as being "the grand promoters of those horrid scenes of slaughter and desolation which, during so many ages, have disgraced the universe."

The imaginative faculty can be political. There was a poiesis of the Luddites and the commons alike which have enabled us to gather Atlantic evidence from 1811–12. Japanese experience has given us Godzilla, a subterranean, terraqueous, and monstrous power, while English experience has given us Ned Ludd, a secular myth of insurrectionary convenience. The war machine and the machines of war, that military-industrial complex, arise from attempts to destroy the world's commons by means of X^2. The only effective antagonist must be the world's commoners with sufficient imagination to see in volcanic eruption, earthquake, and the comet's path the auguries of planetary change and the remodeling of the earth's nations and governments.

-<-->-

---

62. John Charnock, *An History of Marine Architecture* (London: Faulder, 1800).

Also From PM Press & Retort

"This wonderful book, with its faith in the continuity of our radical-communitarian ethic, replants the seedbeds of defiant imagination and hopeful resistance."
—MIKE DAVIS, author of *City of Quartz*

West of Eden

VTOPIAE INSVLAE FIGVRA

Communes and Utopia
in Northern California

EDITED BY IAIN BOAL, IANFERIE STONE,
MICHAEL WATTS, AND CAL WINSLOW

Due to the prevailing amnesia—partly imposed by official narratives, partly self-imposed in the aftermath of defeat—*West of Eden* is not only a necessary act of reclamation, helping to record the unwritten stories of the motley generation of communards and antinomians now passing, but is also intended as an offering to the coming generation who will find here, in the rubble of the twentieth century, a past they can use—indeed one they will need—in the passage from the privations of commodity capitalism to an ample life in common.

"As a gray army of undertakers gather in Sacramento to bury California's great dreams of equality and justice, this wonderful book, with its faith in the continuity of our state's radical-communitarian ethic, replants the seedbeds of defiant imagination and hopeful resistance."
—Mike Davis, author of *City of Quartz* and *Magical Urbanism*

"Utopias—we can't live without them, nor within them, for long. In West of Eden we see California, an earthly utopia, and the Sixties, a utopian moment, in full flower. Brave souls creating a heavenly host of communal spaces on the edge of America, hoping to break free of a world of capital, sexism, oligarchy, race. An amazing place and time that, for all its failures, changed the world—and which finally gets its due in this marvelous collection."
—Richard Walker, UC Berkeley, author of *The Country in the City*

ISBN: 978-1-60486-427-4 $24.95

PM Press was founded at the end of 2007 by a small collection of folks with decades of publishing, media, and organizing experience. PM Press co-conspirators have published and distributed hundreds of books, pamphlets, CDs, and DVDs. Members of PM have founded enduring book fairs, spearheaded victorious tenant organizing campaigns, and worked closely with bookstores, academic conferences, and even rock bands to deliver political and challenging ideas to all walks of life. We're old enough to know what we're doing and young enough to know what's at stake.

We seek to create radical and stimulating fiction and non-fiction books, pamphlets, t-shirts, visual and audio materials to entertain, educate, and inspire you. We aim to distribute these through every available channel with every available technology, whether that means you are seeing anarchist classics at our bookfair stalls; reading our latest vegan cookbook at the café; downloading geeky fiction e-books; or digging new music and timely videos from our website.

PM Press is always on the lookout for talented and skilled volunteers, artists, activists, and writers to work with. If you have a great idea for a project or can contribute in some way, please get in touch.

PM Press
PO Box 23912
Oakland CA 94623
510-658-3906
www.pmpress.org

Friends of PM

These are indisputably momentous times—the financial system is melting down globally and the Empire is stumbling. Now more than ever there is a vital need for radical ideas.

In the four years since its founding—and on a mere shoestring—PM Press has risen to the formidable challenge of publishing and distributing knowledge and entertainment for the struggles ahead. With over 200 releases to date, we have published an impressive and stimulating array of literature, art, music, politics, and culture. Using every available medium, we've succeeded in connecting those hungry for ideas and information to those putting them into practice.

Friends of PM allows you to directly help impact, amplify, and revitalize the discourse and actions of radical writers, filmmakers, and artists. It provides us with a stable foundation from which we can build upon our early successes and provides a much-needed subsidy for the materials that can't necessarily pay their own way. You can help make that happen—and receive every new title automatically delivered to your door once a month—by joining as a Friend of PM Press. And, we'll throw in a free T-Shirt when you sign up.

Here are your options:

- $25 a month: Get all books and pamphlets plus 50% discount on all webstore purchases
- $40 a month: Get all PM Press releases plus 50% discount on all webstore purchases.
- $100 a month: Superstar - Everything plus PM merchandise, free downloads, and 50% discount on all webstore purchases

For those who can't afford $25 or more a month, we're introducing **Sustainer Rates** at $15, $10 and $5. Sustainers get a free PM Press t-shirt and a 50% discount on all purchases from our website.

Your Visa or Mastercard will be billed once a month, until you tell us to stop. Or until our efforts succeed in bringing the revolution around. Or the financial meltdown of Capital makes plastic redundant. Whichever comes first.